A CHAPTER CALLED LIFE

LESSON LIFE TAUGHT ME!!

APURVA MALPANI

This book is a dedication to every single person I have met in my life because they all have taught me about life in some way or the other.

A big heartfelt thanks to NEENA MAJUMDAR of PIAMONY PHOTOGRAPHY for the beautifully clicked cover page. You can follow her on Instagram @piamonyphotography.

I would just say

' Never try to make someone yours. You become theirs and automatically they are yours.'

Contents

Preface

This book is written to let people understand how a different perspective towards anything in life would make you enjoy those moments and face any challenges in life with a smile.
Life is very simple and we tend to make it very difficult with a thought process that has been imbedded in our spirit since childhood.
Everything and everyone that crosses your path teaches you something positive about this life.
Every challenge that we face has a simple answer which we ignore thinking its too simple to work.

Acknowledgements

I acknowledge My Wife Rashmi for being constant support system to indulge in writing.

I would thank my family because without them i wouldnt be here..

I would acknowledge my friends contribution because there advices and problems helped me find the answers..

I would say Thanks to my sis Smriti for helping me out in this book publishing and all tech stuff.

CHAPTER ONE

THE CREATOR, THE CREATION AND THE DESTROYER.

It's a part of conversation between Lord Krishna and Mahamahim Bhishmapitamaha during the war. When Lord Krishna gets angry and says...

"I AM THE CREATOR, I AM THE CREATION AND I AM THE DESTROYER".

"YOU ARE BORN WITH MY PERMISSION, LIVE WITH MY PERMISSION AND DIE +WITH MY PERMISSION"

"WHAT EVER YOU ARE DOING EVEN THE BATTLE IS WITH MY PERMISSION"

"I AM THE MYTH AND THE TRUTH AND THE KNOWLEDGE"

Everyone takes this in literal sense and says that Krishna meant to say he is the GOD and was speaking about it.

But it has a deeper and bigger meaning to it, Decipher it into your present life format and you will get a better understanding of it. It's important to have ability to read between the lines and take learning from it.

SO MY TAKE ON THIS IS...

Every one of us is the creator, the creation and the destroyer... any emotion, feeling or situation that arises in our life is conceived by us, lived by us and destroyed by us. Even the people who come and go in our life is by our permission. The inner fight and the devil with in us is made by us and destroyed by us. Time doesn't heal anything, it's us when we accept the fact and move on or accept there is no way out, the pain subsides or the memory fades.

No one or no emotion can hurt us in our life unless and until we give them the right to hurt us. If a stranger down the road says something vicious we wouldn't care because we do not know that person and nor does we accept the comments by them, so it wouldn't have any impact on us. Remember any bad statement or comment directed towards us, if we do not take it personally it won't have impact on us, because that's something which we did not create so we do not have to live it or destroy it..

If we all accept this one fact that whatever we go through or think about, good or bad is created by us, lived by us and destroyed by us then our life can be sorted so easily. Won't we have very few instances of depressions; the anger would fade away easily and have a clearer picture of life. It's just that we need to give ourselves a little time to think over any decision or promise we make.

Understand that we are the center of our universe and it's up to us to make it beautiful place or a place of conflict. We are the god of our life.

Just believe in yourself and understand we live for happiness so just create happiness in our world.

CHAPTER TWO

THE POWER IN YOU!!

Just think about it,

Out of so many galaxies, there is only one galaxy where we exist! In our galaxy, Earth is just a small part of this galaxy and in this small part, we are one among the billions that live here. We are nothing compared to the bigger picture and yet, we consider ourselves the center of everything. In our world everything moves around US only. Imagine the power we Behold in ourself, we work according to our will and define circumstances as per our will and mood swings. We try to change things around us, like circumstances, people, our goals and dreams with our work and thought process. We put all our energy mentally and physically all around our dream and goal, this leaves an impact on all the people and places surrounding us.

Just imagine that if one person among the billions can do so many wonders in the universe, then nothing would be impossible if millions of them work together (then just think what else can we not achieve.) We can achieve anything we think about by putting our 100% effort and determination into it.

Do you know what is the biggest barrier in our life when it comes to doing or achieving something? It is our thought process! We tend to accept failure easily or play the blame game, because it seems like the shortest way out.

I don't know about our previous life or the next life, because I believe in. living the present life to the fullest. And I just know that I have the power in me to change everything around me and make a better life for the people around me.

I can do the Impossible, because if anyone can do then I can do it too... because there is nothing like IMPOSSIBLE in this life.. like a single person over a decade made a barren land into Greenest Forest.. like a single man for the betterment of his village, single handedly made a road in between the mountain.. I know I can say also do anything!

Because that's the POWER IN ME!!

CHAPTER THREE

ASSUMPTION OF LIFE..

What's there to loose when you don't assume the answer is NO!!

Isn't the assumption of things our biggest mistakes of our life. How many chances have we given up by just assuming things to be out of our bound, by assuming it is a NO even before we trying out. For example, as a student I used to give up on maths thinking or I may say assuming that it's over my head or out of bound of my intelligence.. or like when I was growing up over teenage assuming she won't like me or worst she would say me NO!! Or insult me... or when going for job assuming this job is out of my level or am under qualified for it.

Why is that we assume the negative thinking more than the positive thinking in life , is it because of the fear of loosing or is because of the Ego that will hurt us..

Why can't we just be positive and try to give more time on our weakness and work on it. Why can't we give it a try and learn a lesson from it and not just wait for the food to come served on our plate without working for it.

We should understand that when we assume it as a Negative or a straight NO, giving it a try there is atleast a 50% chances we may get a positive result. Why give up our dreams for someone else thought process or comparing our fate with someone else failure.

We are humans and we grow with each loss or failure or experiences we have in life.

First thing I feel we need to change is take everything in a positive way. Don't see everything we try as failure or loss but instead take it as a step towards learning. Life is all about learning isn't it.

Just look back into your life and see how many dreams, hopes and things we have given up becasuse of our assumptions. Let's start again and try to make those hopes, dreams and things come true now. As the saying goes IT'S NEVER TOO LATE....

Let's change our mindset for a more positive outlook for future... THE RACE iS NEVER OVER UNLESS U HAVE WON IT...

Think about it...

CHAPTER FOUR

ATTACHMENT TOWARDS EXPECTATIONS

Any work you do,

When it's attached to the end results like money, fame, name or happiness then your work and working style gets attached to the result of it. then if you win your arrogance would be increased and make you go towards higher goals with over confidence, and when you lose you get angry and depressed, would make you to lose faith and confidence in your own self.

When it's not attached to the end result then the working style it based upon the nature and capability of the person.

Consider this situation...

If you don't have the pressure and expectation of losing a goal, project or a client and the great joy and happiness of completing it or achieving it... then would the loss or achievement impact you...

No... It won't!! The win or loss would not have impact on your life. It would neither bring sadness nor happiness in your life and your outlook towards other people or your work won't be impacted.

So we can say it's the end result that has an impact on our life. We are so concerned about the end results that our process is changed for the result and it changes us little by little.

But shouldn't we be stable in our life and concentrate on our process rather than results. Because isn't it the fact the results are determined by the process and not the other way around.

When you are concerned about the process without thinking much about the end results it gives you stability in mind and brings calmness inside you. When you are in such a state of mind then any unforeseen problems may arise you would solve it without a sweat, whereas when you are worried about the result and too focused on it either you would overlook small problems or be so unstable that you will lose peace of your mind and still would take long time to solve the problems.

It doesn't mean to stop working with goals in mind... have goals but don't have attachment towards your goal success. End of the day you work with main intention to be more peaceful and happier in life and have a great sleep.

SIMPLEST WAY:

WIN AND LOSS TO BE TREATED EQUALLY, WITH OUT ANY EXPECTATION OF FAME, MONEY, GLORY IF WE DO ANY WORK, WE WOULD BE HAPPY AND CONTENT IN LIFE.

CHAPTER FIVE

THE FIGHT FOR ACCEPTANCE

IN TODAYS Z GENERATION WORLD EVERYONE IS JUST TRYING TO FIND ACCEPTANCE, LIKE IT IS THE MOST IMPORTANT OR JUST THE SOLE THING IN LIFE FOR SURVIVAL....

FROM TRYING TO GET MORE VIEWS ON VIDEOS OR MEMES,

OR TRYING TO GET MORE FOLLOWERES ON INSTA,

TO FINDING MORE FRIENDS ON FRIENDLIST..

LIKE THROWING MOST FANCIEST PARTIEES TO BE THE TALK OF TOWN..

AND THEY SPEND TIME, MONEY OR EVEN HATRED TOWARDS OTHERS JUST TO GARNER MORE VIEWS..

WHATS WITH THIS HAAPPINESS SCHEME WHICH COMES OUT OF OTHERS MISERY..

THE MOST IMPORTANT THING WE ARE FORGETTING IN THIS LIFE IS THAT SELF ACCEPTANCE IS THE ONLY PATH IIN LIFE FOR HAPPINESS AND SUCCESSFUL.. AND WE ARE CLEARLY LACKING IT.

AT PRESENT WE ARE JUST RUNNING AROUND PEOPLE AND WORLD TO FIND OURSELVES BEING ACEPTED AND ATTACHING OUR ALL GOALS TO THAT.. TRYING TO PLEASE EVERYONE AND DO ANYTHING TO JUST BE SEEN AND

FORGETTING THE REAL US COMPLETELY...

INSTEAD, IF WE JUST FIND ACCEPTANCE FOR OURSELVES, AND FIND THE PEACEWITH IN US THE STABLITY WE REQUIRE THEN WE WOULD NOTICE THE REAL MAGIC.. WE WOULD BECOME THE CENTRE OF WORLD AROUND US AND INSTEAD OF WE GOING AROUND THE WORLD WIILL MOVE AROUND US.

WE ARE LIVING THIS LIFE, AND WE SURELY DO NOT KNOW IF THERE WAS A PAST LIFE OR WILL BE A FUTURE LIFE.. SO THE LOGICAL THING IS TO ACCEPT THIS IS JUST THE ONLY LIFE WE HAVE AND LIVE IT COMPLETEY AND MAKE THE BEST OUT OF IT. LIVE IT FULLY EVERYDAY AND EVERY MOMENT. WHY GET BOGGED DOWN BY PAST OR BURDENED BY FUTUREE, JUST LLIVE IN THE PRESENT...

WHEN YOU LLIVE YOUR LIFE COMPLETELY & HAPPILY ACCEPTING ALL AS IT COMES, YOU BECOME CONTENT IN LIIFE & THEN YOU WILL HAVE THAT RADIANCCE AROUND YOU WHICH WILL MAKE OTHERS BE IN AWE WITH YOU.

THE END GOAL IS SAME, THE WAY TO ACHIEVE IS DIFFERENT.

- FIRST IS YOU RUN AROUND THE WORLD, PEOPLE AND LITERALLY BEEG FOR ACCEPTANCE..

- SECOND IS YOU BEING CONTENT AND STABLE BY ACCEPTING YOURSELF AND BE HAPPY AND THE WORLD WOULD ACCEPT YOU...

CHOIICE IS YOURS..

CHAPTER SIX

ACTION AND KNOWLEDGE...

A LIFE MOTTO which I follow or try to follow in my life is...

In future I never ever want to say "I WISH I HAD......"

My journey of life should be like; where I would do all I wished to do which never hurted any one genuinely. Because Regret is something that will haunt us till death.

There are two paths of journey called life...

Path of knowledge and Path of Action...

Both are incomplete without each other.

If you abandon the path of action, your mind would be still actively thinking about the action you could have done with the knowledge you have...

If you abandon the path of knowledge, you would be just wandering around trying various methods like a nomad in a never lasting desert in search of success.

You may get success sometimes just following one path but it's not every time.

Not performing an action after possessing the knowledge or not implanting the knowledge along with action is also an action but a negative one. You act like a helpless ignorant of life...

You are a hypocrite when you have the sense of action to be done or knowledge to be learned but be deluded of understanding and stay static...

Act with the knowledge and belief in yourself, without expecting a victory and just enjoying the process is the true meaning of living a LIFE.

When your action is governed by the unselfishness of achieving worldliness pleasures and just to liberate your mind and soul by doing what you ought to then it brings pure happiness and joy with content in yourself.

Anything you do which enhances people around you or the world makes you attain the highest ecstasy you can imagine.

The pain, sacrifices which we go through to attain the ultimate goal would be more of an enjoying path than a forced path if your journey is more about growing and enjoying it.

The ultimate goal should be growing big within you and rejoicing your own existence and this happens when you are selfless because when you are selfless then only you can accept others in you and grow bigger.

The goals are temporary because it changes or transform into another once you reach them but whereas the journey is constant with small changes. So when you enjoy the journey you not only are happy but the process is etched forever in your mind which makes all other journeys easy...

Never stop growing...

CHAPTER SEVEN

LIVING IN PRESENT AND ACCEPTANCE..

Loss, Defeat, uncertain Time and our careless attitude sometimes put us in trouble and brings us pain and makes us question ourself, our friends and even the God we believe in WHY?? Why Me?? What did I do to deserve it??

We go crazy and make people around us go mad at us... this is a question which cannot be answered at that time, it's like a maze where we are stuck but the simplest way out is not asking why me??, but what should I do now to get out of it... Remember we are not first person out in trouble and there are many people who were in trouble and have come out of it.

We need to grow ourself mentally so big that the trouble and problem looks small in front of us. We need to have a open mind to learn from others without any ego.

Remember the pain of past can be healed in future, and we should not ruin our present with the pains of past but make it the pivot in present to make sure that in future we don't have any such problems..

For example just observe a bird which slowly makes a nest for its family with every single straw of stick or leaves it collect but heavy rains and wild winds break it down into pieces, but the bird doesn't frown or cry over it but just goes back at making a new nest for itself and it's family..

And here we start rue over every small problem or loss in life.. nothing happens in life in just one go, we need to work over it slowly and methodically with just a single intention to do it and not thinking about the results. Because when we are more focused on the results we don't enjoy or experiment the process, we become the robots..

Just let be simple and enjoy the process.. because the process is ur present where as ur start and result are past and future.. if we are more attached or stuck to the past or future we forget to live the present, which we never ever come back..

Life your life looking forward and learning from past but enjoying the present..

Accept the fact that present is the only truth...

Keep smiling and spread the smile..

CHAPTER EIGHT

MY DREAM TO OUR DREAM!!

I will start with a beautiful saying I heard a long time ago.. " If u really wish something from your heart and work towards it, then the whole universe will join in together to make you achieve it."

Don't you sometimes "ONLY SOMETIMES" feel its true..

Every one has dream, to do this or that, to get this or that, but we achieve few and few are left behind as dreams only. Why is it so, why can't all come true even when u feel you have given ur 100% in it.

I believe the dreams which come true are often in which you involve others to achieve it. It's simple let's make all MY DREAM into OUR DREAM.

We need to open up about our dreams to the universe, let them know we are working for it. Tell the universe either to watch it or come be a part of it. We should be open for suggestions and quick tips to help us grow in a much better way. It helps us prepare ourselves for problems that may arise.

Imagine yourself when you are working on organising a small party and imagine if 5 people working together in organising it. U will see oragnising getting easier and with new flow of ideas with different people around and outcome would be even better party than you imagined. When it can be done in small things why not big things.

Believe in yourself and others helping you.

See anyways you gonna achieve your dreams and gotta work on it alone so why not take a chance of letting others get involved in it. It's a try worth taking.

When your dreams are true and of good intentions plus your efforts from ur heart and mind then nothing can stop it to become a reality.

Working to achieve your dreams is like a movie where many characters come and go but what's constant in it is You and your efforts till the end.. Then you can say HAPPY ENDING.

In the end I would say LETS MAKE MY DREAM INTO OUR DREAM.

CHAPTER NINE

THE TRIP TO A TEMPLE..

A trip to temple is divine, blissfull, a bit struggle but a wholesome experience...

I pondered on this particular trip to a temple what is the importance of this whole journey... And learnt a very important lesson it teaches us for life..

The thought about this particular topic led me to a information that maximum temples are on a hilly terrain and with clobbered path, unlike today where u can find ropeway or good decent roads leading to temple.

People usually used to walk up to mountain barefoot whether it's a scorching heat or lashing rains or freezing winter or peaceful spring. And the clobbered path is filled with the rough stones which would be little hurting.

You had to walk all the way to temple and then queue up in the never ending line with requires immense patience to have Darshan. After the few minutes Darshan people usually take a peaceful rest in the temple corridor then move out to small market or "MELA" where they have happiness playing games, buying toys, eating candies and snacks, sometimes even enjoying swings and other rides.

A complete experience

Now let's just focus on different emotions we go through in this one particular journey..

The excitement at the start..

The tiredness in between...

The anguish while in queue for darshan...

The frustration if we get delayed due to some or other reason..

The relief at that moment of darshan..

The rest and peacefulness while u r sitting in the temple complex after darshan..

The joy and nostalgic while moving around the market or mela after wards...

And at last we say everyone Wat a wonderful trip it was

The lesson it teaches is..

Any goal in life is like this journey...

u just need to patient and give ur 100% and never think about backing out in between.. because at the end it's always peaceful content and joyful..

Not only goal even in relationships this entire journey experiences feels to be perfect.

Whats your say.

CHAPTER TEN

A LIFE OF 'U'...

Life .... what does it mean to you.. living, enjoying with friends and family, love, and so on...

But do we really do it...

Isn't present days life a fight between impressing others along with the ambition to succeed more than others and trying to find out our true calling and living a real life...

It's always that we need approval from others for even what we for our heart and soul... like example for me, I knew my passion is writing but to start writing a blog I asked many people how is it and all and shld I start blogging and stuff... Why... isn't it enough that u make ur soul smile abt Wat you doing with ur heart in it... or is it so necessary for the stamp ok it's good by others

Our elders and generations way. back we happy and satisfied and we think it's because of meditation and all... but what is meditation., it's not to correct ur breathing patterns and make u healthy... it's more of knowing yourself... the silence and just breathing away is more to talk to urself... know yourself accept ur flaws and praise urself... close down old windows..

Let's sit down and introspect on ourselves... and let's spread inner smile....

CHAPTER ELEVEN

THE UNCLOSED CHAPTERS..

Imagine entering your bedroom and find clothes spread all around,

Imagine entering your office space in morning and finding all papers kept here and there unorganised...

Imagining in middle of night going to kitchen for a glass of water and not able to find a single glass as all are in sink...

Guess you would be frustrated to the core like I would be definitely...

When we can't bear to stand the unorganised stuff outside our body why do we keep it unorganised inside ourself...

Just find a peaceful place and try to close ur eyes and focus on one particular thing in life... max would 30 seconds by then your mind will wander out to different things about your life...

What are these thoughts... they are the unclosed chapters or books of your life which you have pushed to the back burners thinking when the right time comes will look into it..

Things pile up in back of our mind and that increases the frustration levels and short span of thought process because we have so many things piled up which we haven't answered to yet..

And it's not like that we need to be a yogi or saint to do it... it's our queries and unsolved issues that we need to acknowledge and answer with a simple YES OR NO...

Acceptance is the first step towards answering the problems or dreams then completing it later.. because unless and until we don't give a acknowledgement towards it our mind doesn't move towards answering it..

Happiness is within us.. Accepting to be happy is the first step..

So just close the unclosed chapters of life for a clearer and happier life..

Spread smile

CHAPTER TWELVE

MAKING OTHERS YOURS..

A friend of mine had given me a piece of advice just a month before his death... and which I follow till date...

Never try to make anyone yours., instead you become their and they are automatically urs..

I still follow this because it's such a simple thing... when u let people around you be themselves with you around them (making urself their) they will always want you to be near them (they automatically are urs).

Why do we need to force others to accept our own thought process instead why can't we let them be in their original form and make them feel as if they are speaking to their own soul or own mirror image..

Let's stay original like we were in childhood... and we can be that way only when we make other feel comfortable and be their original infront of us..

Life is to be enjoyed, cherished and most importantly lived. We have been born not stay alone, we will be surrounded by people always (unless u become a monk, that too in complete solidatary) so you need to be such that people accept you like you want them to accept you. Any relation is two ways, wat you give you get.

One thing to remember that not everyone is meant to be part of your life as per your will. But everyone teaches you somethinh in

life, pick the positive things for your own growth.
keep smiling.

CHAPTER THIRTEEN

LOVE...

Love....

Is Love what we say is really love...

Does it have any age that makes it true love...

Does maturity have anything to do with Love and feelings attached to it...

Is it just the bookish definition of LoVe that says Love means only to give and not to expect anything back in return...

Just the LoVe completes our life and brings the ecstasy of life...

Then why there is a feeling of incomplete in Love when you don't get the same kind of Love back....

First of all Love is something which has no right age... it can be at 18 or 80....(talking about lovers love)

Love is blind they say, actually true because when you love someone we just forgoes all negativity and put our soul only to positivity because we feel our love and our desires can never go wrong..

We need to careful the dreams we have dreamt are gonna mark up standards we want in love, it's a dangerous line we have made...

Love is something that makes out something normal into dreamy one in real... dreaming is not bad but expecting it to happen same way is wrong... and that leads to major heart breaks and believing that LoVe is just fake..

Love never knocks on you and say should I happen to you buddy!!! It's just happen in click of the moment and before even u realise it happens...

Love is pure... and love is to give and expect nothing back... the other person may not respond as u like or dreamt of so don't get hurt down... everyone is different... just do ur bit and be happy about it...

And one piece of advice..True Love never have grudges or expectations.. it's just a flow of air that happens and keeps u happy... it's totally on u because it happens to you and neither that u take permission from other person that can I be in Love with you...

Be hopeless romantic but don't attach your expectations to it...

Spread Love...

CHAPTER FOURTEEN

MARRIAGE AND DIVORCE.

I will start this with a beautiful statement I had read somewhere...

A reporter had asked a couple married for 60years "What's the secret of you both being together for so long"

Beautiful answer " We grew up in the age where we mended the things which were broken and not threw them away for new"

Thats the crux of all relation being long and happy..

As the years going by we have seen a number of relationships / marriages being ended are increasing. Ever pondered, why is this happening? What is the reason?

I believe that the next generation will not even believe in the meaning of Marriage !! It would be like just a tag along your name!!

It scares me out... and I partly do believe it's our fault too. Like a small example when our kids play with toys and something get broken we never ever think of fixing it and instead say why do we waste time and buy a new one. Believe me when I say that something like that happened in my childhood and asked for a new toy my Mom would stare at me with devils eyes or if I insist by crying and making a scene I would get slapped. Am happy I had this way of learning life lessons.

TV series , Internet and stuff also has its share in instilling in young people mind that never compromise in anything in life like career, marriage or rights... the whole belief value in purity of marriage has been lost...

As generation is changing we are not even comfortable living with parents and busy in our life professionally so how would our kids learn the value system of mankind which we learned from grandparents. Something to ponder about..

Why don't we all pledge and teach our kids about belief systems of marriage and how to make happy and successful marriage and also standing to our rights. These things we can learn from our parents and grandparents.

CHAPTER FIFTEEN

DREAM OR REALITY !!

Did u ever ponder that the life u r living is really real or is a dream of ur other life...

Hard to ponder and pertain about it...

I have always given my self free time to just think about it, and always felt like I exist in two different parallel life... and it makes me feel worried which is the real life and are those efforts I am putting in it is worth if it's a dream !!!

Is this the life I always wanted in my real life that I am dreaming about.. or is the like a wake up call dream life for me..

I have made my own conclusion in it that wat ever it may be I have to live my life (real or dream) with my sincerity and get the answers from my mistakes and achievements for future reference ...

Life you live at the moment is the only reality whether its REALITY OR DREAM.

CHAPTER SIXTEEN

DEPRESSION!!

26year old, the only son of a business tycoon... having all the luxuries of life... and a life style anyone can envy.. but still feel lonely and is depressed...(because not a true friend and harldy any parent love)

60years old retired and pleasant life.. loving and caring kids and grandkid's... but still feeling depressed... (her husband expired few years back)

34 year old one of the brightest CEO, world travelling job, a perfect family, a great group of friends but still depressed... (His calling was to be a singer which was killed by peer pressure because studies was important)

A young 21 year old, very talented artist and gives all she has in her but rejected again and again due to favourism.. so is depressed.... (no one there to support her and say all will work out)

16year old, perfect happy life with amazing family and siblings is depressed... she recently lost a friend of her

Depression is not due to any particular reason or any particular caste, creed or section. It can strike to most sane person too... it's just like a button pushed in ur brain...

Depression is not something to be ignored or something to be taken just as a mood swing...

Depression can be overcome when you open out or you can help others just by being there for them saying Speak to me...

If you feel something is changed or even if not that just ask people in your closed knit of family and friends "how are you!! Anything I can help! Speak out to me"

This goes a long way...

CHAPTER SEVENTEEN

MENTAL HEALTH AWARENESS...

Is this wat you call about a fight with Depression....

Are we still living in a fog... Depression is not a condition or something... it's a disease... Accept it..

A disease which is even worst than cancer or other things... because it doesn't break you from outside but shatters you from inside...

It takes you somewhere from where you cannot comeback alone and you feel death is the best option for it.. Depression makes you feel the darkest fear of your life is the truth of your life.. it takes you to the place u never intended or wishes to be ever..

A little while ago Sushant Singh Rajput., a star who connected with his fans across the globe in a such a manner that its like loosing your close one... His case proves that no amount of money, luxuries, fame matters in life when you can't speak out your feelings to someone.. Depression doesn't just kills you but first it destroys you completely within then makes you feel that death is the only way out...

A depressed person just need a small support from someone his can call his own or even a stranger to turn over the tide... it's important to speak out your heart.. speak out your thought process.. speak out your fears...

I request you all or actually beg you, don't loose someone you know close because of depression. If you even feel that someone is going through it coax them to speaking out either to someone or they can connect us.. make them do that.. be bad in their books for once by pushing them to this..

I knw this feeling of loosing someone due to #depression, I have lost someone who meant a lot in my life 8years ago.. don't be me...

Spread the words...

Let's fight against Depression..

CHAPTER EIGHTEEN

NEVER JUDGE ANYONE

WHY SHOULD WE NOT JUDGE PEOPLE...

People do judge people involuntarily and some people do judge voluntarily because they wanna boost their self esteem and feel better about themselves...

Few pointers for why should you never judge anyone..

– INCOMPLETE INFORMATION

We often judge without gathering the complete information.. that leads to biased decision and would be harmful to the person being judged and person judging..

NO ONE IS PERFECT

No one is perfect or without any flaws, then what right do we have to judge others on their flaws. Judge yourself first then others..

WE ALL ARE DIFFERENT

Everyone is different like the fingers in our hand... something which we don't do and can't go through doesn't mean others can't.. all are different so respect that

TOLERANCE

Nowadays people do so many things and in so little time and over that they need everything., so they can't just keep calm and quiet. Tolerance is one habit tht you need to inculcate. By this we mean focus more on your problem than others..

NEVER JUDGE A BOOK BY ITS COVER

Need to say anything about it.. I don't think so. It's as simple as walk in the other persons shoes before judging them..

RESPECT

Respect is something we earn and not buy, Respect is a virtue that you earn by respecting all equally. Never judge based on what you respect that thing or that person.. because by judging enemies to make there life miserable we Inturn make out life miserable..

JUDGING A PERSON DEFINES YOU.

When you judge some one it defines your own thought process and your level of dignity ..

All in all never judge someone..

www.ingramcontent.com/pod-product-compliance
Lightning Source LLC
Chambersburg PA
CBHW070531180726
48002CB00022B/2607